*Emma*

# THE REBELLIOUS YEARS

## The Need for Self-Understanding

## PETER MASTERS

SWORD & TROWEL
METROPOLITAN TABERNACLE
LONDON

# THE REBELLIOUS YEARS
## THE NEED FOR SELF-UNDERSTANDING

© Peter Masters 1993
This booklet edition published in 1994
Reprinted in 1998

SWORD & TROWEL
Metropolitan Tabernacle
Elephant & Castle
London SE1 6SD
ISBN 1 899046 04 6

Cover design by Andrew Sides

*Printed in Oradea, Romania by RomFlair Press S.R.L.*

# The Rebellious Years
## The Need for Self-Understanding

*The proverbs of Solomon the son of David, king of Israel; to know wisdom and instruction; to perceive the words of understanding (Proverbs 1.1-2).*

## Secrets of human behaviour

IF WE COULD take in and remember the teaching of Solomon's proverbs, we would be so shrewd! No situation would ever catch us out, and no temptation take us by surprise. Seldom would we be deceived or beguiled by subtlety or cunning, because these miniature parables would prepare us for all the twists of human nature and behaviour.

In approaching this teaching, it is not enough to think in terms of the English word *proverb*, which simply describes a short, pithy statement in general use. The Hebrew term for *proverb* means – a *comparison*, a parable, or an illustration. In the Bible it is translated *parable* on many occasions. It can also mean a *taunting challenge*, and this is the purpose of many statements in the *Book of Proverbs*. They are designed to sting a little, almost to taunt, in order to jolt us into recognising that we are heading in some wrong direction.

The main function of the *Book of Proverbs* is to warn against a pointless and godless life, and to reveal all the depths and secrets of human character and behaviour. Our generation launches young people on to the sea of life completely ignorant of the storms, currents and quicksands which they will soon encounter. But these timeless proverbs equip us so that we immediately recognise different 'characters' or human situations, and are able to categorise them, and know precisely what to expect from them.

Today, however, no one is grounded or prepared for life in this way. Everything has to be learned by bitter experience. We come up through teenage into early adulthood only to be fooled down a wrong path almost immediately. We stumble into harmful situations, and down we fall, headlong. And we are still stumbling through life and burning our fingers in our thirties, forties, fifties and sixties. If only we had been given more shrewdness and insight into human nature at an early stage! This book, the *Book of Proverbs*, has been defined as the best way to put an old head on young shoulders.

It is worth noting that the modern world is deeply prejudiced against the kind of character analysis found in the Bible, because it is offensive to human pride. People like to think of their lives as personal voyages of discovery and accomplishment. They like to think of themselves as totally one-off individuals who possess a very unique blend of views and abilities. They shudder at the idea that their character can be described in a few lines, and their reactions to various situations can be predicted accordingly. Human pride wants to think that we are vastly more sophisticated than this. People recoil from the reality – that 'fallen' human nature is insubstantial, and dominated by its many flaws.

In the *Book of Proverbs* God has compressed a vast quantity of profound insights, casting them in the form of easy-to-remember pictures. Here is the divine genius of God! And yet these proverbs, mighty as they are in Truth, are as handy as a bottle of aspirin, and we can call them to mind in so many of life's situations.

A special feature of the *Book of Proverbs* is the number of times a passage is particularly addressed to the young. 'My son' is a frequent expression. This book has the young in mind as well as the old, and Solomon addresses them with great affection and concern. The *Book of Proverbs* is therefore a highly *sympathetic* book, and in this respect there is nothing to touch it. Solomon wants to protect the young by opening up to them the secrets of life, giving vital warnings and incomparable advice.

## Unique regard for the young

This present society is cruelly unkind to the young, treating them virtually as experimental laboratory animals. Millions of young people are being thrown to the wolves of drink, drugs, illicit sex, and so on, their parents imagining that this is the modern, liberated, reasonable thing to do. Almost the entire younger generation is delivered into the clutches of the millionaire barons of pop, porn and dope, and nobody cares what happens to them.

The young are encouraged to accept as legitimate, and even necessary, youthful, pre-marital sexual adventures, and are taught through magazines techniques for getting maximum satisfaction. Do the arrogant, money-grabbing writers of young people's magazines bother to look into the future and consider the emotional and physical consequences of all this, and the untold suffering to be reaped by thousands over many years? What do they care about the human lives they hurl into the experimental cauldron?

This is an incredibly vicious, selfish, indifferent age as far as the young are concerned. Apart from such matters as heroin and AIDS, there is not a warning to be heard; not a word of real interest in the young. We have to turn to God's Book to find any note of sympathy and care. And in the *Book of Proverbs* we hear it in that deeply touching term, 'My son!'

God cares for the young! 'Come,' says the Lord, 'let Me tell you about human nature. Let Me describe the different character types to you, and warn you about the deeper issues of life, and show you where different actions lead.' That is the *Book of Proverbs* – far kinder than any literature to be found in this sin-sick, chaotic world. We should praise God for His tender and protective love for all, and particularly for the young!

The first verse of the *Book of Proverbs* introduces us to the human author of most of the book, King Solomon, described by the Bible as the wisest and most knowledgeable man in the world, until the coming of the Saviour. But Solomon's wisdom was given by God, and what we find in the *Book of Proverbs* is therefore from God. This is God's infallible analysis of human nature.

Solomon says that his aim is to bring us 'to know wisdom and instruction; to perceive the words of understanding'. These proverbs are devised to enable us to handle life. They show where the traps of sin are hidden, and how to recognise them. They instruct on the 'how to' of decision-making. They teach *skills*.

They are also designed 'to give subtlety to the simple, to the young man knowledge and discretion'. *Subtlety* is craftiness, but here it is meant in a good sense. Young people must be aware that whatever gifts and strengths they possess, and however knowledgeable they are, there is always a degree of susceptibility connected with the early years of life. When young, we are vulnerable to ambush by false ideas and claims, and the *Book of Proverbs* sets out to reveal the morass of deception in this world, and to give shrewdness and discernment.

## The need for self-understanding

The first of the proverbs or parables to be presented by King Solomon goes right to the great mystery of the 'second quarter' of life's journey – the 'rebellious years'. 'My son,' says Solomon, 'hear the instruction of thy father, and forsake not the law of thy mother' *(Proverbs 1.8)*. These words are intended as a miniature parable in which father and mother represent God and His ways, and the hearer represents the human tendency to rebel against God early in life. It applies particularly to younger people, let us say up to the age of thirty. The idea is that self-determination and rebellion surface in the human character in the early years of life, when most people experience a powerful inclination to stop respecting God. This new attitude expresses itself most strongly at some time between mid-teenage and the end of one's twenties.

This has little to do with the chemistry of adolescence, as some people imagine. It is chiefly moral and spiritual. Because we are members of a 'fallen' human race, personal rebellion will soon express itself in an urge to consider 'number one', and to resent all restrictive spiritual and moral values.

It is important to note that this has nothing much to do with whether a person has had a strict upbringing or a permissive one. Where a young person has received a permissive upbringing, that person's inherent rebellion has already been allowed free rein and liberty, and the rebellion will not be so apparent. However, where a person has received a stricter moral upbringing, rebellion will have to fight and struggle for expression. Either way, the rebellion will be there.

Young people between mid-teens and the end of their twenties need to have an understanding of themselves, and to expect the rebellious urge, or life will make fools of them, maiming them morally and spiritually. They need to know that what is happening within them is nothing other than the inevitable activity of a corrupt human nature.

We are certainly responsible for our reaction to this, and will be held to account by God for every sin. But we must not make the mistake of thinking that our urges and desires are the free expression of our original, enquiring minds. They come from a rebellious, fallen, corrupt human heart, which provokes the mind to ask – 'Why can't I do this? Why should I be restrained? Why should I respect this? Why can't I do what I want? Why not? Why not?' Do we know the *real* facts of life – the facts of our *spiritual* biology?

We occasionally hear that some particular make of car or appliance has a 'model defect', which has to be taken account of. Rebellion is the 'model defect' of human beings (except that we brought it about, not the Creator). Even non-religious people frequently come to see this as they get older. They come to accept that human beings are *by nature* cantankerous, rebellious, ambitious, covetous and lustful.

The trouble is that in early life we do not always realise that our strong, rebellious desires for earthly fulfilment arise from the 'model defect' of the human race. We do not know ourselves. We begin to want our own way constantly and strongly, and to seek our own gratification. We begin to pursue leisure and pleasure as if they were the greatest essentials of life; and to seek the applause and approval of others. But we do not understand what is happening within us, namely, that this is all part of the process of rebellion against the Creator and His standards.

Solomon urges insight, awareness and realisation. Young people in particular are urged to be aware of the phenomenon of inner rebellion; to know themselves, and to handle these forces with the help of the Lord.

## *The urge to change our 'values'*

'Hear,' says Solomon, 'the instruction of thy father, and forsake not the law of thy mother.' What is in mind here? Why is there a distinction made between the instruction of one's father and the law of one's mother? In the time and culture of Solomon, most families had their own smallholding, producing their own food, and each family also followed a particular trade. It fell to the father to teach his sons how to run the farm, and also to pass on his trade.

Solomon's parable tells us to listen to the training for life provided by the Word of God, and to take seriously God's reproofs. There is nothing like this available from the world's teachers.

Solomon's plea, 'and forsake not the law of thy mother', provides a beautiful picture, based upon the fact that the mother had the task of instructing the little children at her knee. She taught them the fundamentals; the most elementary laws of right and wrong. She gave them their simplest instruction in spiritual matters also.

Now the trouble with the 'rebellious years' is that we begin to despise fundamental things, often learned in Sunday School, but to some extent known by childhood intuition. These fundamentals are the basic facts that God exists, that He is holy, and that we need to be forgiven. They include the fact that we are not merely animals, but the highest creatures in God's creation, endowed with immortal souls. The fundamentals tell us that there is a Heaven and a hell, and a day of judgement. Also, they teach that God has given the human race a set of moral standards (reflecting His own holy character) which must be obeyed, and which cannot be changed.

If I am a young adult and do not understand that I have a rebellious nature which is bound to assert itself, I will probably assume that my desires to strike out on my own and abandon the training of childhood are my more mature thoughts. I will assume that my earlier beliefs were simpler and less sophisticated than my present ideas.

This is not true – says the proverb. The fact that something was taught to someone *first*, or that it is *simple*, does not make it untrue, or of no value. The first thing everyone does as a baby is to breathe, usually at the first smack, but none of us wants to stop breathing just because it was the first thing we ever did as a baby. Solomon's message is: Don't reject the principles you were first taught. They are your vital equipment for life.

Solomon's appeal to hold on to basic truths about God is reinforced with an illustration. God's message, says Solomon, 'shall be an ornament of grace unto thy head, and chains about thy neck'. The picture here is of a warrior prince who has successfully defended his land and returned victorious. As he enters the capital, a victor's garland is placed around his neck. The garland frames and draws attention to the face, the distinctive, recognisable part of the man, and invites the watching crowds to acclaim him as victor.

The point behind the illustration is that whenever people believe the message of God (the Gospel of Jesus Christ), He transforms their lives, and they possess a distinctive character, and enjoy the presence of the Lord in such a way that people can see that they are different.

## The world's seduction of young lives

Solomon's graphic warnings of the way in which the world entices young lives to reject God and a moral lifestyle begin in *Proverbs 1.10*:– 'My son, if sinners entice thee, consent thou not. If they say, Come with us, let us lay wait for blood, let us lurk privily for the innocent without cause: let us swallow them up alive as the grave; and whole, as those that go down into the pit: we shall find all precious substance...'

The picture here is of a district gang which plans to ambush traders on the highway, some distance out of town. These traders come from other regions carrying precious metals and other merchandise of considerable value. Owing to the absence of modern communications, no one necessarily expects them, and no one in their distant home region knows their exact whereabouts. If the gang overpowers them, they will kill them and bury the corpses somewhere well away from the road, so that it will never be known where or how they met their death.

The invitation to join the district gang represents the trap of sin into which the world lures every young adult. 'My son,' says Solomon, 'if sinners entice thee, consent thou not.' These 'sinners' were once similarly enticed themselves, and from the time of their joining the gang they became the recruiters of others. So it is today. All who are successfully tempted into a life of sin tend to justify themselves by corrupting others. How do the representatives of godlessness go about recruiting others? They offer strong enticements. They dangle benefits before people. They appeal directly to the emerging selfish lusts so active in the rebellious years.

## 1. The appeal of acceptance and approval

Friendship, recognition, acceptance and approval are the first great enticements to a godless lifestyle. 'Come,' is the powerfully attractive word. 'Come with us!' The various representatives of atheism and self-indulgence say, 'Come! We want you. We like you. You are attractive and have abilities. You are a good friend. We need you and we can help you to get on.' The young adult is made to feel so greatly wanted. Here is all the compelling power of friendly enticement.

'If I go with this crowd,' thinks the young person, 'I will be accepted. These people like me. These people want me. These people appreciate me. I will be happy with them.'

By apparent friendliness the world seeks to trap the young on the side of human rebellion, holding pleasure and gain before their eyes. And the attraction of acceptance and recognition to all who are just entering the state of independent adult life, and forming their own identity, is very strong. 'Come, join the gang that mistrusts God and casts Him to one side, and you will have recognition and acceptance.'

## 2. The appeal of liberty from all restrictions

The second enticement to join in the ways of the godless crowd, is the offer of freedom from all restriction and restraint. 'Come over to us,' is the cry, 'and leave your world of repressive rules and moral interference. Taste freedom, and do what you want. Reject the thought that there is a God in Heaven Whom you must seek and serve and love. Come away from the idea that there are fixed moral standards. Break free from the notion that you must keep your body sexually clean, as something honourable. Come away from all that, and join us. Come and do things a different way. Come and do what *you* want.'

How attractive to the young temperament is the call to 'take control of your own life', and experiment with forbidden things!

'Consent thou not,' warns Solomon. Emphatically stand against these luring temptations. Recognise that you are being drawn into a policy of incredible foolishness; into a disastrous trap. Expect that this kind of temptation will appeal to your inherently rebellious heart, and hold out against it, praying to God for help.

## 3. The appeal of an easy time

The third enticement of the world is found in these words of the district gang: 'Come with us, let us lay wait for blood, let us lurk privily for the innocent without cause.' The basic idea of the gang is that this kind of robbery provides a much easier life. All we have to do is arm ourselves and wait for the trading caravan to come through some mountain pass. They do not expect trouble, and it will be so easy to cut them down. Why toil on the family smallholding, or work all your life at stitching tents, when it is so easy to ambush unsuspecting, unprotected traders and discover wealth for a lifetime?

The meaning of the parable is clear, for we hear the tempting voices of this world saying, 'Why spend your life serving God when pleasing yourself and enjoying the world is so easy and so rewarding? This is so easy. This is all pleasure and gain!'

Murder is included in the parable in order to jolt us into seeing that this is a deeply sinful pathway, which will lead us into increasing sinfulness. There is an irreversibility about murder which underlines the indelibility of the guilt of sin, unless God forgives us.

Ambush is selected to show that this is a pathway of much cunning and deceit. 'Let us lurk privily,' says the gang, 'for the innocent without cause.' The parable reminds us that when the world attempts to draw us from the Word of God, it is in order to persuade us to spurn God's rules and laws, and to enmesh us in devious and deceitful ways. This is a *godless* path.

## 4. The appeal of safety from consequences

The fourth enticement of the world is expressed in the words: 'Let us swallow them up alive as the grave; and whole, as those that go down into the pit.' The attraction here, false as it is, is that commitment to the world and to godlessness has no price-tag. It involves no risk, no pain, no disadvantages.

Says the gang, 'The way we shall execute these traders will be quick and clean, and will leave no trace. It will be like swallowing them up alive. You will not have to feel bad about this because their suffering will be short, and we will make sure that the corpses are so well buried that no one will ever find us out. These traders will disappear without trace as though they had never lived, and no one will ever suspect us.'

Today, people say, 'There is no danger involved in abandoning God. Leave that Bible of yours, and all your ideas about religion. Come and enjoy yourself, and do what you like. There is no God out there. There is no day of reckoning. There is nothing wrong in doing what you like with your body and enjoying yourself however you want. There is no final day of judgement. There will be no trouble or blame or shame either now or at any time.

'You need never have pangs of conscience or unrest, once you empty your mind of any idea about God. And this world is a great place to have fun. It will never disappoint you or let you down. Come with us, it is so easy.'

But, as the parable hints, this optimism is naive and ridiculous. Supposing the gang were successful, how would they explain the sudden source of their great wealth to their families? And how would they handle the inner turmoil? Some, if not all, would surely suffer at the thought of those corpses hidden in the ground. And all would be for ever regarded as criminals in their community.

The world constantly lies to the young about the painlessness of sin, and the absence of consequences. Its assurances are attractive, but they are utterly false. Sin must be paid for.

## 5. The appeal of pleasure and wealth

The fifth enticement to join the world is seen in the following claim of the district gang: 'We shall find all precious substance, we shall fill our houses with spoil.'

In other words, they say, 'Come – we shall get possessions we would never obtain through working on our smallholdings, and in such quantity! We shall have all we want.'

The world uses similar arguments in its efforts to wrest young people from God. 'Forget God and the Christian life and you will have pleasures and possessions and experiences you would never know as a believer in God. You will have the things *you* want, and as much as you like, all the time. As an unbeliever, unrestrained by any thought of God, and any worry about sin, you will be able to live entirely for yourself. You will be free to promote your interests and try anything you want. Nothing need be wrong for you, and nowhere out of bounds.'

The lure of a godless lifestyle can seem tremendously appealing when the rebellious years come. Do we understand the great battle for our minds and hearts when we pass through the second quarter of life? On the one hand, there is the sympathetic, merciful call of the message of God, while on the other is the trap of sin, with all its baits. Do we see the dangers of the rebellious years, when fallen human nature begins to express itself so powerfully?

## 6. The appeal of solidarity

The sixth enticement to throw aside faith in the Lord, and to join the world, is seen in the call of the district gang: 'Cast in thy lot among us; let us all have one purse.' We may amplify their words a little to get the sense: 'With us you will have security and peace. We will look after you. Give us your money, commitment and time, and we will be as one person.'

Just as friendship and acceptance are of special importance to the young, so are security and solidarity. More than at any other time of life there is a need to be in step with peers and in line with fashions. Many younger people experience their worst terrors on being seen to be different from the majority in some way.

'Come with the crowd,' says the voice of the world. 'Be like everyone else. Do what everyone is doing. Here you will be alright, and secure. We will not only be your friends, we will look after you as well. We will not laugh at you, deride you or attack you, because you will be one of us. Give yourself to us, and be safe.'

It is a lie, of course. All too soon something goes wrong in life and the person who has trusted the world finds that all the comradeship evaporates. Our friends get married and so do we, and we lose touch with most of them. Our 'circle' gets smaller, and our burdens greater, and what other people think becomes less important to us. But in early years it can seem so important that we may sacrifice even our morals and our belief in God to keep in with 'the crowd'. Solidarity, or 'fitting in', is an appealing fraud to which countless people surrender.

These are the arguments and appeals pressed on to the minds and hearts of young men and women to trap them into a life leading away from God, and into selfishness and sin. 'My son,' appeals Solomon, 'walk not thou in the way with them; refrain thy foot from their path.'

Note the emphatic, urgent tone of his words. He seems to say, 'Do not take that path! Do not even try it for a few years. If you say, "I will try the world for a time, and then weigh things up," you will find yourself trapped. It is all too easy to join the gang, and almost impossible to leave it.'

'The overtures of the world are a deadly trap,' hints Solomon, and he knew, because he fell into that trap for years before the Lord worked in his life to set him free.

'Their feet run to evil,' he says. They have not thought through their policy at all, nor its consequences. They run down that road, blinded by prejudice and driven by a desire for sin. They have not looked ahead to see what really happens to others who take that road. Their rejection of God is the most ill-considered act imaginable. Don't you do it! Turn back! Seek the Lord, and find Him. 'My son, if sinners entice thee, *consent thou not*' *(Proverbs 1.10)*.

May God save us from naive unawareness of our vulnerability in the rebellious years. May we recognise the stirrings and the tantrums of the fallen human nature within us. When we understand ourselves, and what causes us to be the way we are, then we can approach the Lord in the right spirit, and seek forgiveness and conversion. Our rebellious inner nature does not excuse our sins, but it draws us down an unbelieving, selfish, sinful pathway, and there is no greater tragedy than a young man or woman who thinks that these urgings are the product of their free minds.

If we have already yielded our lives to the Lord Jesus Christ, and now walk with Him, and know Him, let us not be swept away when the old nature tries to reassert itself. And if we have not yet turned to God, let us trust God's Word alone for a true analysis of our nature and our needs. We should remember that we are the privileged possessors of immortal souls, and be moved to seek the Lord before we become too hardened and corrupted to care.

## Companion booklets by Dr Masters:

### How to Seek and Find the Lord

The author shows how we must respond to the message of salvation, defines belief, and describes the right attitude in which to approach the Lord.

### The Cruelties of Atheism

This booklet shows the motive for atheism, explains why it is unreasonable, and then shows its dishonest methods, its 'agenda', its failure to improve people's lives, and its immensely cruel results.

## Magazine format booklets:

### Answers to Questions 1

Includes articles answering – How can I be sure there is a God? Why does God allow wars, sickness and tragedies? Were we designed or did we evolve?

### Answers to Questions 2

Includes articles answering – Why are there so many different religions? What exactly is conversion? How could a God of love send people to hell?

### Unseen World

Includes articles entitled – Time the Mysterious Dimension; Is Death a Conscious Experience? and Waveband of the Soul (how to pray).

Further details, together with information about audio and video cassettes of messages by Dr Masters, may be obtained from:

Tabernacle Bookshop, Metropolitan Tabernacle, Elephant & Castle, London SE1 6SD. E-mail: Bookshop@MetropolitanTabernacle.org